Rae Armantrout

MADE TO SEEM

NEW AMERICAN POETRY SERIES: 20

LOS ANGELES
SUN & MOON PRESS
1995

Sun & Moon Press
A Program of The Contemporary Arts Educational Project, Inc.
a nonprofit corporation
6026 Wilshire Boulevard, Los Angeles, California 90036

This edition first published in paperback in 1995 by Sun & Moon Press
10 9 8 7 6 5 4 3 2 1
FIRST EDITION
©1995 by Rae Armantrout
Biographical material ©1995 by Sun & Moon Press

This book was made possible, in part, through an operational grant from the
Andrew W. Mellon Foundation, through a production grant from the
California Arts Council and through contributions to
The Contemporary Arts Educational Project, Inc.,
a nonprofit corporation
Some of these poems appeared in the following magazines:
A•bacus, Avec, Big Allis, Conjunctions, Grand Street,
Furniture, o•blĕk, O/Two: An Anthology, Screens
and Tasted Parallels, Shiny, and Verse. The author
wishes to thank the editors of these magazines and anthologies.

Cover: Jean Baptiste Siméon Chardin, *The Skate* (detail)
Cover Design: Katie Messborn
Typography: Guy Bennett

LIBRARY OF CONGRESS CATALOGING IN PUBLICATION DATA
Armantrout, Rae (1947)
Made to Seem / Rae Armantrout
p. cm – (New American Poetry Series: 20)
ISBN: 1-55713-220-8
I. Title. II. Series: New American Poetry series; NAP 20
PS3551.R455M3 1995
811'.54–dc20
94-49732
CIP

Printed in the United States of America on acid-free paper.

CONTENTS

SIT-CALM

In the excitement phase
we think we want something
we're made up to seem
exaggeratedly unfit for,
say, touch.

This is the funny part,
but also the dangerous
moment. Right away
we're talked out of it–
no harm done–
by a band of wise-acre friends.

"I don't know
what I'm thinking," we say,
to a spike of merriment.
Here is the warm,
human part
which dissipates tension

RETRACTION

1

Incongruous, you wish!

Do you think
you can put everything back
where it belongs
and impress the management
with your long memory
and good intentions?

2

Interest disguises hope.

Out the window
two junipers are twitching
back and forth in sync
behind the palm which,
I now see,
is also moving.

3

Slap-happy fronds, that kind of revision.

Now, when it makes no sense,
I'm at the center
of the dispelled universe,
"snapping to"
too often—as if there was
nothing but

ONE REMOVE

Right off
the tip of your tongue.

You don't know
what, but
hold its place.

It must be where
you're not wrong.

*

"That's happened
to me," I coax,

but you suspect
a bait-and-switch

and so hold
off.

COVERS

The man
slapped her bottom
like a man did
in a video,

then he waited
as if for shadow
to completely cover the sun,

Moments later
archeologists found him.

*

The idea that they were reenacting something
which had been staged in the first place bothered
her. If she wanted to go on, she'd need to ignore
this limp chronology. She assumed he was con-
scious of the same constraint. But she almost
always did want to proceed. Procedure! If only
either one of them believed in the spontaneity of
the original actors and could identify with one. Be
one. For this to work, she reasoned, one of us
would have to be gone.

*

"Well, look who missed
the fleeting moment,"

Green Giant gloats
over dazed children.

If to transpose
is to know,

we can cover our losses.

But only
If talking,

Formerly food,

Now meant
Not now

So recovery
Ran rings.

If to traverse
is to envelop,

I am held
and sung to sleep.

THE CREATION

Impressions
bribe or threaten
in order to live.

Retreating palisades
offer
a lasting
previousness.

*

Let us
move fast
enough, in a small
enough space, and
our travels
will take first
shape, then substance.

*

In the beginning
there was measurement.

How much
does self-scrutiny
resemble mother-touch?

*

Die Mommy scum!

To come true,
a thing must come second.

BUILDING

Growth is "winding down."
I must deal with this

block by block.
An odd assortment, but…

There's someone familiar
in a beauty shop,

wearing protective gear,
idly twisting

a wooden spigot
shaped like an electric chair.

A person might be startled
by seeing handiwork.

A student is learning
"to care and not to care."

MY PROBLEM

It is my responsibility
to squeeze
the present from the past
by demanding particulars.

When the dog is used
to represent the inner
man, I need to ask,
"What kind of dog is it?"

If a parasitic
metaphor grows all
throughout–good!
Why stop with a barnacle?

A honeysuckle,
thrown like an arm
around a chain-link fence,
would be far more

articulated,
more precisely repetitive,
giving me the feeling
that I can go on like this

while the woman
at the next table says,
"You smell pretty,"

and sends her small daughter's
laugh, a spluttery orgasm,
into my ear–

though this may not have been
what you intended.

It may not be a problem
when I notice
the way the person shifts.

THE SIGNS

Planetesimal:
round but homeless,
a man sits cross-legged,
dabbing at pale skin
with cupped palms
as if bathing,
being bathed.

*

A skyful of
faded primaries:
Big Bear's and Chevron's
exemplary rectangles
are more mood than substance–
kindergarten stuff.
They join the white horizon
flawlessly.

INCIDENCE

Our mother
who turns
sights to instances
gave us this
ground, our
sense of before
and behind.

*

On a blank sign
shadows might be the features
of a murdered child.

Crowds are amazed
that a picture appears
unsponsored. This
is jubilation.

Crews stop the gap
with a memorial
to reduce the risk
of incident.

*

We start
where shadows strum the wall
over a crib.
Why attend
absence's modulations?

A PULSE

Find the place
in silence
that is a person

or like a person
or like not
needing a person.

*

After the heart attack
she fills her apartment
with designer accents–

piece by piece.

*

This is a bed,
an abiding
at least,

close to *lastly*
but nicer.

*

Light changes:

Separation
anxiety refers
to this

as next
tears itself off.

*

A hospital calendar
shows the sun going down
on an old-time,
round, lime-green
diner.

*

Just a quick trip back
to mark the spot
where things stop
looking familiar.

RELATIONS

Mirroring the stricken,
we pose as decoys.

*

Modulating vertigo,
moths

are an orgy
of relative proximity.

An electron gun
incites a screen to glow

and there we are
"very optimistic"

as if memories
were prepared responses

and partners
good hosts.

*

And it was
back to business,

inventing contexts
to explain away

waves of inflection.
"Take a look,"

says the Bombshell
to the Emperor
on the beach
of a crumbling island.

"Not at me, you idiot,
at the shape the country's in!"

SETS

"You can stop dancing now, Launch-Pad!"

One's known
and one knows better
in the perfect sentence.

The all-new
short-list.

The extra-terrestrial
is made to appear
as a ballerina,

a flamenco dancer
and a disco stud
in succession.

The flustered magician
claims he was prepared
for this "eventuality"

and, of course, he was.
His each miscarriage
is a ticked off item.

A vivid memory
is frightening
because it makes time
short, being one of few.

This is Extra-Classic!

SPANS

The kids are excited
by the prospect

of the finite: seed packets
in the garden shop,

a magic number
of distinctions,

the upcoming
              recital.

*

The mother
dreams her thoughts

have parted company
and become innocent:

pine, grass and wind.

*

A bird folds her wings
and drops

one stitch
to decorate the past–

thus touchingly
real,

      extant.

NATIVE

How many constants *should* there be?

The slick wall of teeth?

The white stucco
at the corner,

flag on its porch
loosely snapping?

*

"Get to the point!"

as if before dark–

as if to some bench
near a four-way stop.

*

At what point does
dead reckoning's

net
replace the nest

and the body
of a parent?

*

The apparent

present.

Here eucalyptus
leaves dandle,

redundant but syncopated.

MAKING IT UP

What do you call it
when men dress up
as barber poles:
a different century
or an ice-cream parlor
full of crying kids?
A father hit one and said,
"I didn't touch you."

So her dream is a scape, not world.

*

His bike resting against it,
a man perched on a bus stop bench
playing a wooden flute
as if making a claim
were its own reward.

Today she likes those
for whom it's clear
how they've made peace
and with what.

*

As if "candlestick" accounted
for the length of the pimple–
curiously curved or carved.

Now she says that's impossible.

Then she remarked
to her dream guests
how odd it was
for a new, natural form
to resemble a man-made one.

CROSSING

1

We'll be careful.

Repression informs us
that this is not our father.

We distinguish
to penetrate.

We grow and grow,

fields of lilies,
cold funnels.

2

According to legend
Mom
sustains the universe
by yelling
"Stay there
where it's safe"
when every star
wants to run home
to her.

Now every single star
knows
she wants only
what's best
and winks steadily
to show it will obey,
and this winking
feels like the middle
of an interesting story.

This is where
our history begins.
Well, perhaps not
history, but we do
feel ourselves preceded.
(Homeostasis
means effortlessly
pursuing someone
who is just
disappearing.)

3

Now here it is
slowed down
by the introduction
of nouns.

Eastwood, Wayne
and Bogart:

faces
on a wall in Yuma
constitute
the force required
to resurrect
a sense of place.

(Hunger fits
like a bonnet
now, something
to distinguish.)

4

On the spot, our son
prefaced resorption, saying,

"You know how we're a lot alike…"

He couldn't go out
on that day, but
he could have a pickle.
Out of spite, he crawled
to the kitchen, demonstrating
the mechanics of desire.

5

The sky darkened
then. It seemed
like the wrong end
of a weak simile.
That was what shocked us.
None of our cries
had been heard,
but his was.
When something has happened
once, you might say
it's happened, "once and
for all." That's what
symbols mean
and why they're used
to cover up envy.

THE KNOWN

The cat sniffs the bookshelf, and her knowledge of
its smell is punctuated then by a gingerly present
tense, relatively more acute, I guess, as time is
than eternity.

There is something stately about it. To ring is
stately. I am someone and everyone has something
solemn to tell me. One of us has died. I say I didn't
know her well–which is what I always say.

A dog's bark whooshes by, looming large on the night-
time or suddenly anonymous street. I could be disqualified
for writing, "suddenly"–or could have been "if the
truth were known." It's the job of the poem to find
homes for all these noises.

KINDS

I 'm just soaking up all
this *nurturing*,"
one stressed–

so a noun
is a kind of scab.

*

Leaf still
fibrillating on the vine;

watch it closely
for a minute

as if listening
to a liar.

*

Bird–trills break
into droplets,
then *rise*–

so beauty's a residue
of banished desires?

NEXT

Self-reflection:
a watery drama
tonight on
                end.

A fountain?

Is it there?

Is it him?

Is he moving?

Here a dream answers
"Yes" or "No"
to her invisible
captor.

Does it matter
if the probes
are unmotivated
                hoots?

Dreamed I doubted what I heard.

Dreamed what was called
mannish, wasn't.

Dreamed there was trouble
about a drawer, about understanding
its contents.

Dreamed I was rummaging
through the top drawer
of Madonna's bureau,
searching for a claim check.

Hey, everybody needs somewhere
in which to present
the drama of their limitation.

Is it upcoming?

Is it collapsing?

Will something
double for it?

TAKING STEPS

You'll be
the expanse I'm facing:
petroleum frills
on aluminum poles
for Xmas,
good soldier Chevron pumps,
then the more
tentative flag,
the fence
and the flowery,
foreign jacaranda.
       Hazy
hosts of unfillable
rank. Sheer direction–
so that I'm always
passing up

A STORY

Despite our infractions
we are loved
by the good mother
who speaks carefully:

"I love you, but I don't
like the way you lie there
pinching your nipples
while I'm trying to read you a story."

Once there was an old lady who told her son she
must go to the doctor because she was bleeding
down there. She didn't look alarmed, but suppressed
a smile, as if she were "tickled," as if she were
going to get away with something.

"Look," said the doctor, "you are confusing
infraction with profusion. *Despite*
may be divided into two
equal segments: Exceptional and Spiteful."

But the stubborn old woman just answered,
"When names perform a function,
that's fiction."

THE DAFFODILS

Upon that inward eye

> A wig and eyelashes
> made of pipecleaners
>
> affixed
> to a rear-view mirror
>
> which says,
> "Flapdoodle!"
>
> in a commonsense, country way
> that just reflects

The bliss of solitude

> and baby shoes
> attached by a red tube
>
> to the small, plastic
> blades of a "chopper":
>
> this never-ending lineup
> of spontaneous abortions

could have begun
with a singing crab

whose embarrassment
when brought before the king

was one way
to placate matter.

VISIBILITY

1

I have to go for a check-up. In the examining room I'm surrounded by windows looking out on busy streets. The doctor assures me these are one-way. In the dream, it is attractive to be deceived.

2

Because of his name, I'm afraid this doctor's silences won't be well-modulated. Motivated? The invisible barricades won't be in the right places, and I won't be able to maneuver around them, neatly, in the roadster I don't have–which is *supposed* to be funny!

3

It's strange to see traffic backed up at this checkpoint–people scattering–heading for the hills or darting across the freeway toward the beach. There are words connected with this scene. "Aliens" is one. If I can avoid these words, what remains should be my experience.

STATES

In an amusement like the past,
I'm superior to knowledge
and can label broad lapels
"tokens of transvestism."

Then someone's nose is
"cute as a button," but
in the futuristic sense,
as one extols
rapid transit
dropping citizens at nightspots.

Here I protest
the corny names
of destinations like "Dreamland."
Still, at dawn it's clear
the seedy club
is, in fact, the state of being–

where a man masturbates
in front of a mirror
and I don't know
the first thing,
don't know the difference
between greed and seeming.

Now one hopes
that peace, descending,
isn't "a blessing,"
but a token.

TURN OF EVENTS

Outside it was the same as before, scrawny palms and oleanders, their long leaves, ostensible fingers, not pointing, but tumbling in place–plants someone might call exotic if anybody called–and the same birds and hours, presumably, slipping in and out of view. She kept coming out onto the porch with the sense that there was something to it. Perpetuation and stasis. She wanted to deal with the basics–though what this scene might be the basis for she didn't know.

This was her native tongue, slipping in and out of order–its empty streets and loose, flapping leaves, its bald-faced simplicity as if a way had been cleared for something huge. Shape was the only evidence. She went back in. She should think about how the house was built or how it was paid for. How a feeling can have a shape for so long, say an oblong, with sun falling in a series of rhomboids on its wooden strips. It would have an orientation. She wondered whether there was much difference between orientation and reason. She would sit facing the door.

THE WORK

1

Forever drawing water through a maze of
cabbages?

From dreams and memories, words vanish first.

Now any old gizmo will serve as the pratfall.

Sunlight falls across the boards as a gift box,
the way screens fall on pedestals.

On one show, he won her love by guessing
what she'd like to eat:
coconut and mashed potato clumps awash in milk.

Sleep engenders novelties by inducing conviction.

Already the sense of this as a new and
distinct day is wearing off.

2

Evenly spaced
on the heavenly floor,

those hairy stalks
do not object

to duplicating
one another's work.

This is creation's
diligence

in which we
stand apart.

NORMAL HEIGHTS

We just assumed
that our relations were mere
happenstance, insignificant–

that there was a secret order
nullifying this one.

*

We had been asked to listen
to *Little Women, Little Men,*

a hoard of diminutive
and dated instances.

A preemptive "Yes, but…"
was the model of balance.

*

Columnar
palms and junipers swayed
toward or away from one another;

this would only look like
relaxation
for a few moments.

*

We weren't supposed to stare
so, when we did,
a blankness spread across
the once pleasant features.

We got started:
lists of objects, lists of attributes.

*

We were just playing
(cross-words or Scrabble)
for what seemed like years,
waiting for the speech to resume.

We weren't supposed to mind
losing.

CONFIDENTIAL

Shooting pleasures
Ok'd by
My being seen
For
Or as
If.

*

Not just light
at the end of the tunnel,

but hearts, bows, rainbows–

all the stickers
teachers award if pleased.

*

Pigeons bathe in technicolor
fluid "of a morning."

*

If I was banging
my head with a shoe,
I was just exaggerating–

like raising my voice
or the ante.

Curlicues
on iron gratings:

Can it be
a flourish is a grimace,
but a grimace isn't a flourish?

*

On the inscribed surface
of sleep.

Almost constant
bird soundings.

"Aloha, Fruity Pebbles!"

Music, useful
for abstracting emphasis.

Sweet nothing
to do with me.

MAPPING

1

At the upper end, the businesses seemed more distinct,
each with its own style, or character understood as
pretense, flaunting the energy pretense expends–thus
light-hearted.

2

The airplane cruised between buildings like an intelligent
missile. The issue wasn't terror, but character, how
each passenger responded individually. One matched her
levity to the captain's.

3

"Ride that thing!" a man whispered, then, "Keep me informed!"
This bothered her and it was her job to find out why. She
concluded stylized ejaculations were obscene, but there was
more. It wasn't like him to repeat a formula, seemingly
beside himself while, in fact, stationed above.

YOU

1

Simple
identity of slack
wires with shadows
on a white wall,
god-like
in the long pause.

2

When the boy who
sees a snapshot
can't get in
through remembering,
he must ask his mom
"What were *you* thinking?"

LEAVING

The urge to wander is
displayed
in a spate of slick,
heart-shaped leaves.

*

Cellophane grass and
foil eggs.
            The modesty

of standard presentation
does remind me of home
sickness.

*

As if some furtive
will's receded
leaving meaning
in its place:

a row of coastal
chalets.

*

With waves
shine slides over
shine like skin's
what sections
same from same.

*

Coarse splay
of bamboo
from the gullies,
I write,
as if I'd been expecting
folds of lace.

*

Mine was about
escaping Death though
Death was stylized, somehow,
even stylish. So was I!
So I was hidden
among fashionable allies.

NEW AMERICAN POETRY SERIES (NAP)

For a complete list of our poetry publications
write us at Sun & Moon Press
6026 Wilshire Boulevard
Los Angeles, California 90036